THE ALICE KRAMDEN GUIDE TO HANDLING A HARD-HEADED HUSBAND

Peter Crescenti

Rutledge Hill Press

Nashville, Tennessee

Additional material and compilation copyright © 1992 Peter Crescenti

Photographs on pages 16, 46, 50, 81, 92, 100, 102, and 120 courtesy of Personality Photos, Inc., and used by permission.

Published in Nashville, Tennessee, by Rutledge Hill Press, Inc., 513 Third Avenue South, Nashville, Tennessee 37210.

Typography by D&T/Bailey Typesetting, Inc., Nashville, Tennessee
Design by Harriet Bateman

Library of Congress Cataloging-in-Publication Data

Crescenti, Peter.
    The Alice Kramden guide to handling a hard-headed husband/Peter Crescenti.
       p. cm.
    ISBN 1-55853-176-9
    1. Honeymooners (Television program) 2. Husbands — Humor. 3. Kramden, Alice (Fictitious character) 4. American wit and humor. I. Title.
PN1992.77.H623C62   1992
791.45'72 — dc20   92-15788
                                    CIP

Printed in the United States of America
1 2 3 4 5 6 7 — 97 96 95 94 93 92

To

Marvin Marx & Walter Stone
Leonard Stern & Syd Zelinka
Herb Finn & A. J. Russell

The men who put the skin on the bones
and the words in the mouths
of the funniest characters
in television history.

**A sincere "Thank You" to all those
who helped make this book possible:**

Larry Stone and Ron Pitkin, Rutledge Hill Press
Howard Berk, Viacom
Denise Marcil, Denise Marcil Literary Agency
MPI Home Video and CBS Video Library
Mike Nejad, photographer
"Daddy" and Howard Frank, Personality Photos Inc.

"Blessed is the man who trusts in the Lord,
whose confidence is in him."
Jeremiah 17:7

CONTENTS

INTRODUCTION

Alice Kramden!

The Joan of Arc, the Florence Nightingale, the Marie Curie of wives!

Poor Alice, the wife of Ralph Kramden.

Awe and pity. Those are the contrasting sentiments that come to mind every time I think about Alice Kramden. Who would argue that this woman is worthy of anything less than our highest esteem for spending the best years of her adult life baby-sitting Ralph Kramden, Brooklyn's answer to Moby Dick, Genghis Khan, and the Little Rascals all rolled into one?

But even as I admire the virtues that have made Alice a heroine for the ages — her patience, her wisdom, her wit, her levelheadedness, her ability to function without a single electrical appliance — my heart swells with compassion for her as well. You would be less than human if you could not feel pity for a woman who spends her days and nights feeding her husband one minute and letting out his pants the next; who is left at home alone — without television or a telephone, remember — while he bowls, shoots pool, and carouses at the Racoon Lodge, and who scrimps and saves pennies from his meager salary only to watch him throw it away on crazy get-rich-quick schemes like uranium mines in New Jersey and glow-in-the-dark shoe polish.

Yes, Alice is one in a million all right. That's too bad, too, because there are probably 999,999 carbon-copy Kramdens running around out there. But that's where this book comes in.

Finally, for every woman who has had to deal with her own home-grown despot comes help from the ultimate source: Alice Kramden! *The Alice Kramden Guide to Handling a Hard-Headed Husband* is a manual for marital warfare, a book crammed with wisdom and experience, strategies and techniques learned in the trenches — in this case a dingy two-room flat in Brooklyn.

The Alice Kramden Guide contains battle-tested insults, wisecracks, and head-ringing zingers that are guaranteed to stop the most boorish, self-centered husband in his tracks. How can we be so sure? They derailed Ralph Kramden — what better proof do you need?

From all-purpose cracks suitable for any occasion to ammo for women who are married to men whose egos are matched only by their waistlines, *The Alice Kramden Guide* will, in the immortal words of Alice herself, help turn your Richard the Lion-Hearted into a Richard the Chicken-Hearted!

As a bonus there are reinforcements too: Alice's mother and her best friend, Trixie. When you see how mercilessly Mrs. Gibson manhandles Ralph, you'll get the idea that Alice's razor-sharp wit may have been passed along to her in her genes. And for those wives whose husbands are more dopey than despotic, you'll enjoy the choice words Trixie has for her husband, Norton.

So this is it, from Alice Kramden to you, the book that is guaranteed to turn any King of the Castle into just another lowly peasant.

THE ALICE KRAMDEN GUIDE TO HANDLING A HARD-HEADED HUSBAND

A PLACE FOR EVERY HUSBAND AND EVERY HUSBAND IN HIS PLACE

Ralph: You don't know how to handle money.

Alice: Of course I don't. I never had any practice.

16   A PLACE FOR EVERY HUSBAND AND EVERY HUSBAND IN HIS PLACE

Ralph and Alice are arguing about money.

Ralph: I don't want my salary to leak out.
Alice: Your salary couldn't drip out.

The Kramdens and Nortons are visiting a bus company executive and his wife.

Ralph: When Mrs. Weedemeyer comes out it might be good if you complimented her on how she decorated this place. She might give you a tip on how to fix up our place.
Alice: I could sure use her help. I just can't make up my mind what color pan goes best under our icebox.

Ralph has cheated to win a contest.

Alice: I don't want to be any part of this. This whole thing sounds like a fraud to me and I'm not gonna get involved in it.
Ralph: What's the matter with you, don't you want a nice boat trip?
Alice: Yeah, but I'd like to go across the ocean, not up the river!

Ralph's male ego is showing again.

Ralph: Men run this world, Alice. Men! They're responsible for the shape the world's in. Men!
Alice: Well I'm sure glad to hear one of you admit it.

Ralph is on a rent strike and the landlord has cut off the utilities.

Ralph: Washington at Valley Forge didn't have any conveniences either. He was fighting for a cause the same way I am. I'm exactly like Washington at Valley Forge.

Alice: Not exactly, Ralph. George did not have Martha with him.

If they ever institute a Nut-of-the-Month Club.
I've got a very good idea who's gonna be January
and February.

Ralph tries to butter up Alice.

Ralph: I was thinkin' it over and I realized that it was a long time since I got you any candy. Can you remember when I got you the last box of candy?
Alice: Ralph, you didn't buy any more of that phony oil stock?!?

Ralph needs money to pay his lodge dues.

Ralph: Please, Alice, do you know how embarrassing it would be to be thrown out of the Racoon Lodge?
Alice: Certainly. It's pretty embarrassing just to be in it.

Ralph has bragged that he knows Jackie Gleason, and now he has to find a way to get him to the Racoon Lodge dance.

Ralph: Boy, don't you realize there are some times in your life that you gotta take a chance? Where do ya think we'd all be right now if Christopher Columbus didn't take a chance?
Alice: We'd be in Italy and you'd be telling everyone you knew Gina Lollobrigida.

Ralph has to see the bus company psychiatrist.

Ralph: I've got news for you, Alice, big news. Your husband is crazy.
Alice: All right, what's the big news?

Ralph thinks he's being honored by the Racoon Lodge.

Ralph: Do you realize that when I become Racoon of the Year that we will have the privilege of free burial in the Racoon National Cemetery. Do you know where it is? Bismarck, North Dakota!
Alice: That's just wonderful, Ralph, I've always dreamed of going out west. In fact, with the chance of being buried in Bismarck, North Dakota, I just can't make up my mind whether I want to live or die.

Ralph is dreaming again.

Ralph: You're not gonna discourage me, Alice. I'm loaded with ideas.
Alice: Anybody ever hears any of those ideas they'll sure think you're loaded.

Ralph insists that he has to bowl with his team shirt.

Ralph: How're they gonna know I'm a Hurricane?
Alice: Just open your mouth.

Alice strikes again.

Alice: I didn't have to marry you, Ralph Kramden. I was already engaged to somebody else when I met you.

Ralph: I happen to have met that no-account bum that you were engaged to. Why didn't you marry him?

Alice: Everybody thinks I did.

Ralph wants money to buy a do-it-all kitchen gadget and then sell it on TV.

Ralph: Look, how long do you think it would take that guy to sell two thousand of these if he went from door to door?

Alice: About one minute if this was the first door he knocked on.

The Racoon Lodge is going broke.

Ralph: If I don't get some money into that treasury, you know what might happen? The Bensonhurst chapter of the Racoon Lodge may no longer be. Do you know what that means?
Alice: Yeah, real estate values in Bensonhurst will go up a hundred percent.

Alice gives Ralph a history lesson.

Ralph: Men have done all the great things since the beginning of time. Give you a perfect example. There'd be no America if it wasn't for Christopher Columbus.
Alice: There'd be no Christopher Columbus if it wasn't for his mother.

Ralph wants money to rent a costume for a Racoon Lodge costume ball.

Ralph: If you can't give me ten I'll take five. For five dollars I can go as Billy the Kid.
Alice: I tell you what I will do. I'll give you a tin can and you can go as Billy the Goat.

Ralph's spent the evening flattering Rita Weedemeyer, a co-worker's sexy wife.

Mrs. Weedemeyer: What a husband you have. He certainly is a *trea-sure.*
Alice: A trea-sure. If he keeps this up much longer he's gonna be a *buried* treasure!

Ralph has bought Alice a used vacuum cleaner.

Ralph: Put this on for cleanin' rugs.

Alice: We haven't got any rugs.

Ralph: Put this on for cleanin' upholstered furniture.

Alice: We haven't got any upholstered furniture.

Ralph: Clean drapes with this.

Alice: And we haven't got any drapes.

Ralph: And this picks up the dirt.

Alice: That we've got.

Alice wants to go out with Ralph.

Alice: You never take me out.
Ralph: I never take you out! What about your birthday?
Alice: I hardly call watching you bowl a night out!

Ralph thinks he's hit the jackpot.

Ralph: You're not discouraging me. This time my ship is coming in.

Alice: Listen, Ralph, if I have to wait any longer for your ship to come in, I'm gonna have to join the longshoreman's union.

Ralph's boss is coming for a visit and he's splurged on refreshments.

Ralph: Don't you get the psychology of this thing? Whaddya think he's expectin' to get? Some tutti frutti ice cream, a couple of cookies and maybe some bon bons. Instead, what do I throw at 'im? Champagne, caviar, and Havana cigars. Whaddya think he's gonna think?

Alice: He'll think you haven't been ringing up all the fares.

The vacuum cleaner Ralph has bought for Alice doesn't work.

Alice: You're wasting your time Ralph, this is nothing but a piece of junk.
Ralph: Is that so? What are you, an authority on vacuum cleaners?
Alice: No, I just happen to be an authority on junk.

Alice won't release the purse strings.

Ralph: You scrimped and saved? What about me! I haven't bought anything for myself that wasn't an absolute necessity in the last five years.

Alice: Well what about the bowling ball that you bought last month? I suppose that was an absolute necessity?

Ralph: It certainly is. You can't bowl without it, can ya?

Alice doesn't want Ralph to go bowling.

Ralph: The Hurricanes need me.

Alice: Well, then I feel very sorry for the Hurricanes because the biggest wind of them all ain't gonna be there!

Alice questions Ralph's sanity.

Alice: I think you should have your head examined.

Ralph: I'll have it examined, Alice. Any doctor, any place, any hospital. They could bring doctors from the moon down here to examine my head. And they'll find nothing in there, Alice!

Ralph is entering contests.

Ralph: Here, look at this one. Twenty-five words or less why I like Krinklie Winklies and I'm off to Europe on a luxury liner. Finish this Clean-O jingle and I'm off to Hawaii. Here's another one, find the hidden faces in the trees and I'm off to Sun Valley in my own car.

Alice: You keep up this raving and you'll be off to Bellevue in your own straitjacket.

Ralph threatens to hock the furniture.

Ralph: I'll get the three hundred dollars, Alice. I'll get the three hundred dollars if I have to sell everything in this house.

Alice: Well, that's a good start but where're you gonna get the other two hundred and eighty?

Ralph thinks he can be a hit songwriter.

Ralph: I got this piano so I could be a songwriter. Can you tell me one thing that a person could do to make more money than being a songwriter?

Alice: Yeah, selling pianos to idiots who think they can write songs.

Ralph and Alice play "Can You Top This."

Alice: That is the dumbest thing that anybody has ever said.

Ralph: That's the dumbest thing that anybody's ever said? That's the dumbest thing? How about the time I said "Will you marry me?"

Alice: How about the time I said "Yes!"

Ralph's in a panic because the guys at the Racoon Lodge think he's getting Jackie Gleason to host their annual dance.

Ralph: You didn't see how excited they were when they found out that I knew Jackie Gleason. They were so excited that the president bought everybody a round of drinks. Do you know the last time the president bought everybody a round of beer?
Alice: Yeah, the time you told them you knew Rudy Vallee.

Alice agrees...Ralph's the boss.

Ralph: I'm the boss, you're nothin'! The boss. B-o-s-s. I'm the boss, you're nothin'!
Alice: Big deal. You're the boss over nothin'.

Ralph wants to crack open a bottle of wine.

Ralph: Drinking doesn't affect me.
Alice: Oh no?!? Then how about the time we ate in that Hungarian restaurant. You had a two-day hangover from a slice of rum cake.

Alice critiques the Kramdens' furnishings.

Ralph: Are you trying to say that you think you might have done better?

Alice: I didn't say that, Ralph, but all I know is my sisters don't live the way we do. Agnes has got a perfectly beautiful apartment done in Modern. And Grace's place is just beautiful and it's done in Early American. And Helen's place is done in French Provincial. What period is this place done in Ralph, Early Depression?

I am the only girl in town with an atomic kitchen. This place looks like Yucca Flats after the blast.

Ralph and Norton have first-row seats for the fights.

Ralph: I'm not missin' the best fight of the year!
Alice: Listen here, you try and walk outta that door and you'll be *in* the best fight of the year!

*Ralph's the manager and Norton's the bellhop in a
dilapidated hotel they've bought.*

Ralph: You keep that up and you won't even be a
bellhop in this hotel. I'll make you a…uh…
Alice: Why don't you make him a guest, nothing could
be worse than that.

Ralph has tickets to the World Series the same day Alice's sister is getting married.

Ralph: I am goin' to see the ballgame!
Alice: The only way you're gonna see that game is if they got television in the hospital.

Ralph takes command.

Ralph: A man's home is just like a ship. And on this ship I am the captain. You are nothing but a lowly third-class seaman. Your duties are to get the mess, swab the deck and see that the captain feels good. [Alice starts to leave.] Where are you going?

Alice: Seaman Kramden, third class, is reporting to the poop deck until this big wind blows over!

Ralph feels unwanted.

Ralph: All you ever think of me as is a machine or somethin', a workhorse! A slave! You care more for anything in this house than you care for me. If you gave me as much attention as you gave that plant, I'd be satisfied.

Alice: All right, from now on I'll water you three times a week.

A hotel Ralph and Norton have bought is a disaster area.

Ralph: All it needs is a little cleanin' up and we got plenty of time to fix it too 'cause we don't have to have this place fixed until the highway's built.

Alice: I think it'd be easier if they fixed up the hotel and we built the highway.

A PLACE FOR EVERY HUSBAND AND EVERY HUSBAND IN HIS PLACE

Ralph wants better lunches.

Ralph: Look, the human body is like a machine. It's gotta have the right fuel or it won't run. I'm not gettin' the right fuel in my lunchbox.
Alice: All right, Ralph, you'll get fuel. Tomorrow I'll stick a lump of coal in your lunchbox.

Ralph thinks Alice's mother is coming for a visit.

Alice: What am I supposed to say when my mother comes here and you're not here?
Ralph: What do I care what you say? Tell her I ran off and joined the circus.
Alice: What as, an elephant?

AND THEY SAY ALL FAT MEN ARE JOLLY

Ralph: Don't tell me what to do. I wear the pants around this house.
Alice: Believe me, those pants would fit around this house.

50   AND THEY SAY ALL FAT MEN ARE JOLLY

Ralph may be too fat to drive a bus.

Ralph: For your information, for my height I'm four pounds underweight. It says so in the chart.
Alice: You must've been looking at a chart for a hippopotamus.

Ralph recalls his days as a Romeo.

Ralph: There were plenty of girls crazy about me and you know it. Every time I went down to the beach they used to crowd around me.
Alice: Sure they crowded around you. That didn't mean they were crazy about you. They just wanted to sit in the shade.

The Kramdens debate Ralph's eating habits.

Alice: We'll go to Mother's, eat supper, and come right home.
Ralph: Now you know I'm not that kind of a man. I'm not the kind that eats and runs.
Alice: Eats and runs? The way you eat you're lucky if you can walk.

Alice wants to go fishing with Ralph.

Ralph: What do you know about fishing in the first place? When did you ever catch anything?
Alice: Fifteen years ago. I caught three hundred pounds of blubber.

Ralph is complaining that Alice has more clothes than he does.

Ralph: Why is one pair of my pants in that drawer?
Alice: Because one pair of your pants is all that'll fit in there.

Ralph's burned his finger and Alice has given him butter to soothe it.

Ralph: Butter on my finger at eighty-nine cents a pound?!? Will you stop throwing my money around. Isn't there any lard here?
Alice: Yeah, about three hundred pounds of it.

Ralph's threatening to leave Alice.

Ralph: Just remember, you can't put your arm around a memory.
Alice: I can't even put my arms around you.

Alice hasn't sewn Ralph's socks.

Ralph: Did I or did I not ask you when I left the house this morning to please sew my bowling socks?
Alice: I'm sorry, Ralph, I meant to sew them but I've been awful busy.
Ralph: Whaddya mean, "busy"? What could you have that's more important to do? What could be a bigger job than sewing my socks?
Alice: I was sewing your pants.

Ralph thinks he's more financially secure than Norton.

Ralph: I've got one thing that he hasn't got. I got it here!
Alice: You got it here. And you got it here. And you got it here!

The wife of a bus company executive is discussing nicknames.

Mrs. Weedemeyer: Don't you have certain names you like to call your husband?

Alice: I have several I'd *love* to call him.

Mrs. Weedemeyer: All you have to do is pick your husband's outstanding feature and find a name that fits.

Alice: Oh, I see. Isn't that a good idea, Tubby?

Ralph thinks he's being promoted at the bus company.

Ralph: It doesn't look like I'm gonna need this lunchbox much longer.

Alice: Ralph, you're going on a diet.

Ralph: No, I am not goin' on a diet!

Alice: Then why won't you need this lunchbox? Are you getting a bigger one?

Alice is planning Ralph's birthday party.

Alice:...potato chips, peanuts, chocolate cake with "Happy Birthday to Ralph" on it. On second thought I better make that coconut cake.

Trixie: Why? Ralph's crazy about chocolate cake.

Alice: That's just it. I bought him a new belt for his birthday and I want to make sure it fits the day after.

Trixie: Well, you could always exchange it for a larger size.

Alice: There is no larger size!

I suppose you've forgotten that all this stuff has to go back too. All, that is, except your suits, Ralph. The tailor can't take those back. He doesn't know any elephants that need a new wardrobe.

Ralph tries to explain how he got stuck between two steam pipes in the basement.

Ralph: It wasn't my fault, Alice, it wasn't my fault.
Alice: No, it wasn't your fault, Ralph. You were just doing an impersonation of two pounds of baloney in a one-pound bag.

A theatrical producer has been building up Ralph's ego.

Ralph: One night at rehearsal he said that I have something that comes across the footlights and reaches out into the audience.
Alice: You certainly have!

Alice gives Ralph a lesson in current events.

Ralph: That's the trouble with you, you don't know the latest developments.
Alice: I don't know the latest developments? Who is it that lets your pants out every other day?

Alice won't fund Ralph's scheme.

Ralph: I want that money!

Alice: You're not gettin' the money, I'm savin' it to buy furniture.

Ralph: Furniture? Furniture? We got furniture!

Alice: I would like to have at least one comfortable chair in this house. The only thing we have now that is overstuffed is you.

The cost of living is killing Ralph.

Ralph: Maybe your sisters have got better apartments than we have. But I happen to know that I've got more expenses than their husbands. I've got more expenses than all of them put together.
Alice: That's right, Ralph. They get their suits at Bonds. They don't have to go to the Fat Man's Shop.

Ralph's into another scheme.

Ralph: This is probably the biggest thing I ever got into.
Alice: The biggest thing you ever got into was your pants.

The Kramdens have a difference of opinion.

Ralph: That's the difference between you and me, you are gullible and I'm not. You're the type that would bend way over and pick up a pocketbook on April Fool's Day. I wouldn't.
Alice: You couldn't.

Ralph wants a vote of confidence.

Ralph: Other husbands do things and they can always be assured of their wife standing behind them. Why can't you stand behind me?
Alice: It's not my fault, Ralph. There just isn't enough room back there.

Alice "needles" Ralph.

Ralph: Whaddya doin' with all that material, makin' a bedspread?
Alice: No, I'm letting your pants out again.
Ralph: Don't you think you let 'em out a little too much?
Alice: I haven't started yet.

Ralph can't stand his diet.

Ralph: I don't need to diet anymore, I lost a pound.
Alice: Ralph, when you lose a pound it's like Bayonne losing a mosquito.

Ralph's a contestant on a TV quiz show.

Alice: I'll be very proud if you win the six hundred bucks.
Ralph: Six hundred dollars! Peanuts, peanuts. What am I gonna do with peanuts?
Alice: Eat 'em, like any other elephant.

The Kramdens and Nortons have gone out together.

Trixie: On the bus there are just two empty seats. And who sits in those two empty seats?
Alice: Ralph.

Ralph shares his unfulfilled dreams.

Ralph: All my life I wanted to be something in the sports world. I wanted to play baseball but I was too slow. I wanted to play basketball but I was too short. I would've given my life to be a jockey but I was a little too heavy.
Alice: A little too heavy?!? You're too fat to be a horse!

Ralph won't take his doctor's advice.

Alice: All I know is, the doctor says you gotta take some weight off.
Ralph: Is that what he says? Well I drive a bus all day, I gotta have some food that sticks to my ribs.
Alice: To the inside of your ribs. You've been piling it up on the outside.

Ralph plans to force his boss to give him a raise.

Ralph: I'm gonna squeeze Mr. Marshall. He's in no position to squeeze me.
Alice: Of course not. He couldn't even get his arms around you.

Alice prepares dinner.

Alice: I'd better get Ralph's supper started 'cause he'll be home any minute.

Trixie: Whaddya havin'?

Alice: I got succotash left over from Tuesday night, red cabbage from Thursday, and meat loaf from last night.

Trixie: Gee, Ralph must like meat loaf to eat it two nights in a row.

Alice: Oh no, he can't stand it. Think there'd be any leftovers if he liked it?

Alice wants Ralph to give up bowling.

Ralph: Why should I cut out bowling? It's my only relaxation. Besides the exercise is good for me to keep down my weight.
Alice: You don't need anything to keep your weight down. You need something to hold it up.

Alice wants a telephone and Ralph is against it.

Ralph: The bills'll get bigger and bigger and I'll get less to eat. I'll start losing weight. Then do you know what I'll look like?
Alice: Yeah, a human being.

Norton has a sleepwalking problem.

Alice: Trixie hasn't had any sleep in three nights. If she doesn't get some rest soon she's gonna waste away to nothing.

Ralph: How about me? I haven't slept in three nights! Don't you care if I waste away?

Alice: Yes, I care, Ralph, but you wouldn't waste away if you stayed awake for nine years.

Ralph's advice has cost Norton his job, and now Ralph wants to get it back for him.

Ralph: There's nothin' Alice, nothin' in this world that's gonna stop me from goin' down that sewer tomorrow morning.
Alice: Oh no? There isn't a manhole in this city that you could fit through.

Alice is cutting Ralph's hair.

Ralph: Watch out with that scissors. One wrong move, I could lose an ear.
Alice: So what? The way you eat you'd grow another one.

Ralph has helped capture a criminal.

Ralph: I'm big news, Alice. I'm a hero, a hero, a heee-rooo! Do you know what a hero is?
Alice: Yeah, it's a fat sandwich that's fulla baloney.

MOTHER KNOWS BEST

Ralph: One of these days you're gonna push me too far.
Mrs. Gibson: The only thing that could push you is a bulldozer!

Alice's mother has the last word.

Ralph: There isn't room in this place for you and me.

Mrs. Gibson: There isn't room in this place for you and anybody!

Alice defends Ralph.

Mrs. Gibson: Every time I come over here something else is busted. If only that husband of yours would buy you something new for once.

Alice: Mother, it isn't Ralph's fault.

Mrs. Gibson: It isn't Ralph's fault! Look, Alice, just because you're married to a horse doesn't mean you have to live in a stable.

Ralph has brought home a suitcase he found on the bus.

Alice: What's in it?

Ralph: I don't know what's in it. It can't be anything of value or they woulda claimed it.

Mrs. Gibson: It can't be of any value or you wouldn't have found it.

Ralph is complaining about Alice's mother picking on him.

Ralph: I suppose it was my imagination the day we got married and she went around the reception telling that joke about me to everybody.
Alice: What joke?
Ralph: You remember the joke. She ran around to everybody sayin', "I'm not losing a daughter, I'm gaining a ton."

Alice gets a present.

Alice: Oh Mother, a dress! How did you know? It's just what I needed.
Mrs. Gibson: Well it wasn't hard to figure. When you're married to Ralph Kramden you need everything.

Ralph's is a case of unmistaken identity.

Mrs. Gibson: Hello Ralph.
Ralph: Hello. How'd you know it was me?
Mrs. Gibson: I could feel the floor sag.

Ralph has been arguing with Alice about whether he should "go all the way" on the TV program "$99,000 Answer."

Mrs. Gibson: I hope you go on to the "$99,000 Answer."
Ralph: Oh. Well Alice, I gotta admit that now and then your mother shows a small tiny bit of wisdom.
Mrs. Gibson: As a matter of fact, I can't wait to hear you answer that question. I wanna see the expression on your face when you miss it!

What's that, your lunchbox?

A prowler is roaming the neighborhood.

Alice: You're gonna stay here with me. I'm too nervous to go to bed and I'm not gonna stay up all by myself.

Ralph: Well, if you want somebody to stay up with you, get your mother. She'll protect ya. She knows how to handle a man that sneaks in at four o'clock in the morning. Ask your father.

Alice needs a new stove.

Mrs. Gibson: If that husband of yours didn't waste all of his money on these get-rich-quick ideas he could buy you a new stove.

Alice: Well, Mother, new stoves cost a little more than we're prepared to spend right now.

Mrs. Gibson: Yes, I suppose that you can't buy a new stove and a Geiger counter all at the same time.

Alice's mother knocks the Kramdens' appliances.

Mrs. Gibson: When I got married I had a more modern stove than that to cook on.
Ralph: When you got married fire wasn't even invented.

Mrs. Gibson thinks Alice is underfed.

Mrs. Gibson: Alice, you look sick. Are you getting enough to eat?

Alice: Of course I am, Mother. You wouldn't say that if you could see our food bill.

Mrs. Gibson: I don't doubt the bills are high, but how much of the food are you getting?

Ralph thinks his mother-in-law's coming to visit.

Ralph: When she comes here I know what she does. She starts right in with the wisecracks. "Poor Alice hasn't got a washing machine. Poor Alice hasn't got an electric stove. Poor Alice hasn't got a vacuum cleaner." You call your mother and tell her she can't come.

Alice: I can't. Poor Alice hasn't got a phone either.

A LITTLE HELP FROM TRIXIE

You can take the man out of the
sewer, but you can't take the
sewer out of the man.

Alice and Trixie salute their husbands.

Trixie: Alice, a toast. I give you our husbands.
Alice: A toast. You can have 'em.

Trixie needs a favor.

Trixie: Alice, I cleaned out my refrigerator and it's defrosting now. I was wondering if you'd go up tomorrow morning and turn it back on for me.
Alice: Oh sure.
Trixie: I'd ask Norton to do it for me but every time he looks into an empty icebox it makes him cry.

Norton's jealous because Alice has kissed Ralph and Trixie hasn't kissed him.

Norton: Whattsa matter with me, Trixie, don't I get nothin'?
Trixie: I'm too tired.
Norton: How d'ya like that? I been workin' down the sewer all day and she's tired.
Trixie: That's *another* reason.

Norton doesn't want to take Trixie to the Racoon convention.

Norton: She was away with me once on a trip. Boy, she was on my neck all the time, naggin'. I couldn't go bowlin', I couldn't shoot pool, she just ruined everything.
Ralph: When was that?
Norton: On our honeymoon!

Ralph tells Norton to ignore Trixie's call to come home from the pool room.

Norton: What's gonna happen to me when I get home?
Ralph: I'll tell ya exactly what's gonna happen. When you get home Trixie'll be standin' there, glarin' at ya.
Norton: Yeah, and I'll be duckin'.
Ralph: No you won't, you'll just stare right in her kisser and say, "Make me some ice coffee."
Norton: Then I start duckin'.
Ralph: You don't have to duck because nobody's gonna be throwin' anything.
Norton: Then I must've walked into the wrong apartment.

Alice and Trixie bemoan the way their husbands treat them.

Trixie: What's happened to their manners anyway?
Alice: Don't you know? They swapped them for a marriage license.

Alice encourages Trixie.

Alice: Ed'll make everything come out right for you. He's pretty smart.

Trixie: Yeah, he's smart, all right. He was in the seventh grade so long they named a seat after him.

Trixie tells a "dirty joke."

Norton: Hey Trix, what are all the potted plants doin' in the bathtub?

Trixie: Well, this morning Mrs. Manicotti gave me some extra ivy she had and I couldn't find any place else to put 'em.

Norton: What am I supposed to do, take 'em out every time I wanna take a bath?

Trixie: Will it hurt ya once a month?

Whoever said the Age of Chivalry was dead was right, and I know the two guys that killed it.

Norton goes "off the record".

Reporter: In your house who is the boss, you or your wife?

Norton: In my household, I am the boss of the household. I think that any man that is afraid of his wife is not a man. I can't stress this point too strongly, that a husband is the boss. Now don't quote me because if my wife reads that she'll kill me.

Norton is hosting a party for his co-workers.

Trixie: Alice, you won't believe this, but Ed's gonna tell all the guys from the sewer to come formal.

Alice: Formal?

Trixie: White tie and black boots!

Norton has been locked in his apartment in a rent strike.

Norton: I never spent such a miserable three days in all my life. I didn't mind being cut off with no heat, electricity, hot water. But being locked up with Trixie for three days is more than I can stand!

Trixie's no Emily Post.

Alice: When Trixie serves dinner does she serve it from the left or from the right?
Norton: Neither. She just says, "It's on the stove, get it yourself."

Trixie reminisces about Norton's love letters.

Trixie: In one letter he had a dilly I'll never forget. It went, "Since I met you, my sewer has become a Tunnel of Love."
Alice: Wow!
Trixie: Don't laugh, Alice. That's the line he won me with!

Ralph's advice on how to handle Trixie has backfired.

Ralph: I don't know what could've gone wrong. I gave you the whole routine what to say.
Norton: Look, don't blame me, I knew my lines, it's just that Trixie didn't know her part.

Alice and Trixie can't get used to their husbands' new manners.

Trixie: You think you got it bad. Wait'll I tell you what my Ed did. Two o'clock this morning he wanted to get a drink of water, so he wakes me up so he can tip his hat before he leaves.

Norton won't take a hint.

Trixie: Ed always forgets our anniversary. One year I tried something to give him a little reminder. Two weeks before I sent him a note. It said "Your wedding anniversary is in two weeks," signed "A Friend."
Alice: What happened?
Trixie: A few days later I got a note. It said "Mind your own business," signed "A Husband."

A prowler has been seen in the neighborhood.

Alice: Ed, you shouldn't be down here at a time like this, leaving Trixie all alone upstairs. She must be terribly frightened.

Norton: Don't worry about Trixie, she can take care of herself. A stranger on the street once bothered her, got fresh with 'er. She smacked him over the head with a pocketbook, chased him for six blocks.

Ralph: She catch 'im?

Norton: She sure did. That's how we met.

ALICE'S GREATEST SPEECHES

*Ralph is angry because Alice hasn't ironed his
bowling shirt or sewn his socks.*

Ralph: I know why you haven't got any excuse Alice.
You're afraid to give me an excuse because you know
that I know that you know that I know what you been
doin' around here all day...sittin' there foolin' around!
Alice: You know something, right after you left the
house this morning I got into one of those silly moods
of mine, you know how I get sometimes? So just for
laughs I thought, "Well, I'll do the breakfast dishes and
make the beds and take the garbage down." Then
when I came back I was still in such a funny mood I
thought, "Why should I settle down to the drudgery of
mending your socks," so I scrubbed the kitchen floor.
Then you know something, I was still so giddy and so
gay over this whole thing that I thought I'd really
enjoy myself, so I washed all the windows. Then,
Ralph, I went out and did the marketing and I came
back with a pot roast and I put the pot roast on the
stove and while it was cooking I went in and cleaned
out the bedroom closet. Now I know that this may
sound like work to you Ralph, but it isn't...it's fun!
Good sport! Do you know why it's such good sport
Ralph? Because I'm so loaded with modern
conveniences, just loaded. Steam irons and vacuum

cleaners and dish washers and washing machines, to say nothing of this lovely new modern refrigerator. Oh, that reminds me, it's time to defrost it. *[Alice removes the pan from under the icebox and empties the water into the sink.]* That will give you a rough idea, Ralph, of what a joy it is working around this apartment all day. You know why? Because it's so up to date. I am the only girl in town with an atomic kitchen. This place looks like Yucca Flats after the blast!

Not at all impressed with the amount of work Alice has done, Ralph threatens to give her "demerits" every time she doesn't do something he's told her to do.

Alice: Don't you try to bully me, Sgt. Kramden. I have got plenty to do around this house all day and you know it. You come home after working an eight-hour shift and you're absolutely exhausted. Do you know how many hours I work a day, Ralph? Twenty-four hours a day, seven days a week and I haven't had a day off in fourteen years. Holidays are a double shift. Now let me tell you something, there's an old, old saying, Ralph: "Man works from sun to sun, but woman's work is never done."

Ralph: Good gosh!

Alice: I'll tell you why a woman's work is never done Ralph, because she's got the toughest boss in this whole world — a husband!

Now Alice raises the ante by insisting that the Kramdens hire a maid.

Alice: Don't you worry Ralph, you won't have to pay her. I'll pay her. I'm gonna get myself a job and for once in my life I'm gonna take it easy. I'm gonna get one of those "sun to sun" jobs Ralph, and I'm gonna come home at night and the maid will set dinner on the table, then she'll do the dishes and it'll be just like having a vacation.

Ralph: Oh, it'll be a vacation, heh? Workin' for some boss will be a vacation, heh? Well I'm callin' your bluff, go ahead and get a job. I'll be happy to have a maid around here, then maybe I'll get somethin' done!

Alice: Ha ha, you think a maid is gonna jump at your slightest whim?

Ralph: She certainly will. I happen to be the *master* of this household!

Alice: Har har hardy har har!

Alice has tried to rekindle the romance in the Kramdens' marriage by preparing a gourmet candlelight supper, but boorish Ralph has done nothing but grouse. Finally, Alice loses her patience.

Alice: I tried, Ralph, heaven knows I tried, but you are impossible. I thought I could have things a little different around here for a change — candles on the table, tablecloth, full-course meal for you. I even tried to dress myself up to look a little more attractive for you. And what are the thanks I get Ralph? None, absolutely none! Oh boy, when I think of what I've had to put up with! Fourteen years ago I got married, Ralph Kramden, and what did I marry? I don't even know I've got a husband. One night you and Norton go out and shoot pool, another night you go bowling. Then there's always lodge meetings, steamed-clam bakes, shuffleboard, skeeball tournaments, political things. One thing after another, Ralph. You've never spent one single evening alone here with me. Not one! Well, I've got news for you, Ralph. I suppose I shouldn't complain about all this. There's no reason for me to complain, because although you're never home Ralph, and although I'm not married to you because you're married to Ed Norton and I'm married to these four walls here, while you're out you leave me those little sweet mementos to remember you by. Like the shirts that I gotta wash and the socks that I gotta mend and your pants that I gotta let out three times a week! *These foolish things,* Ralph, remind me of you! Well, that'll give you a little picture of it Ralph. That'll give you a nice tidy little picture of what it's been like for me married to you for fourteen years. The all-American boy! But maybe it's my own fault, Ralph, for not stopping this when it got started. After all, I did have a warning, sure I had a warning. I should've known what I was in for, Ralph, when you took a *bowling ball* along on our honeymoon.

Now Ralph, who has been simmering while Alice has been blowing off steam, responds.
Ralph: Are you through? Are you finished?!? Are you done, completed?!? Well, now let me tell you a few things. You certainly have it tough around here, ha ha ha! You got a lot to complain about! All I know is, when you wash my shirts you never have to wash more than one — I'm wearin' the other one! I suppose I oughta compliment ya on the way you darn my socks, heh? Take a little look at that! *[Ralph removes his shoe and reveals his toes sticking out of the front of his sock.]* Don't you talk to me about complain', strugglin' and workin'. Heh, you kill me! Whaddya think my life

is, a picnic or somethin'? Whaddya think I'm doin' while you're around this forced labor camp all day? Did you ever drive a bus in front of Klein's on a sales day? Did you ever have four hundred women charge your bus like there were no other kinds of transportation? And out of that four hundred women how many do you think have the right change? One! And she's on the wrong bus! Of course it wasn't always as tough as this. It was a little easier before when the fares were ten cents. They weren't satisfied with that, they had to raise the fares. Did they raise it to somethin' easy, like fifteen cents? No, thirteen cents! I gotta play around with pennies all day! Do you know there's a penny ward in Bellevue for bus drivers? And they got a long waiting list and I'm on the list! You think it's any fun on the bus tryin' to explain to people that there's a rear to the bus? And then I come home here and instead of gettin' a little solace and consolation, what happens? You gotta start in that I can't go bowlin' and I can't play pool. Then you gotta talk about my skeeball tournaments. Well, for your information Mrs. Wisenheimer, it was the prizes that I won in the seekball tournament that practically furnished this whole apartment. And that little snide remark you make about the pie-eating contest, it just so happens that the gift certificate that I

ALICE'S GREATEST SPEECHES   **109**

won in the pie-eating contest got you the very dress you're wearin' right now! All I know is, I won the pie-eating contest and you got the dress. What've I got to show for it? *[Alice looks square into Ralph's belly.]* Don't you dare say anything!

Ralph is a contestant on a TV quiz show and he's made up his mind that he's going to win the jackpot. Alice is trying to bring him back down to earth.

Alice: Ralph, will you please be sensible. They don't *hand you* the $99,000, you gotta answer questions, and they're very tough questions.

Ralph: I know what you're tryin' to say Alice. What you're tryin' to say is your husband is too dumb to answer any questions. Well, that's where you're wrong. And for your information a twelve-year-old kid on one of these programs walked in and answered a $16,000 question. Twelve years old she was! Stands to reason to me, a grown man, I must be able to answer the same questions that a twelve-year-old kid can answer.

Alice: Spell "antidisestablishmentarianism".

Ralph: I'll spell it…I'll spell it….

Alice: Well, go ahead.

Ralph: I'll spell it when you give me $16,000 for spelling it!

Alice: Sixteen thousand for spelling it? I'll give you $32,000 if you can say it!

Ralph is trying to convince Alice to help fund his latest get-rich-quick scheme, a kitchen gadget he wants to sell on television.

Ralph: Alice, I don't want the money. It's not for me, it's to get you things. You can get the television set you want, the washing machine you want, you can get the vacuum cleaner you want.

Alice: Ralph, you don't have to get me any of those things, we got 'em already.

Ralph: Whaddya talkin' about, we got 'em?

Alice: Sure, there's our television set over there. Don't you remember, Ralph, that's the one you bought out of the profits of that sure-fire investment, remember? The new invention that was gonna do away with electric lights? Wallpaper that glows in the dark! There's our vacuum cleaner right over there Ralph, isn't it a beauty? You know how we got that? I bought it just as soon as the money started rolling in from that other investment of yours that couldn't miss...the uranium field in Asbury Park! And we don't need a new washing machine Ralph, that one over there is just fine. Do you remember the scheme that got us that one? No-cal pizza!

Alice has had a talk with Judy Connors, one of the neighborhood teens, and it has inspired her to try to "recapture her youth". But when she suggests to Ralph that they go out rollerskating and to a dance contest, Ralph ridicules her idea and humiliates her in front of Norton.

Alice: You can stop laughing, Ralph. If you wanted to make me feel ridiculous you've done that, Ralph. I admit it, I made a mistake, I was trying to be something I'm not. At the same time Ralph, I didn't think it was so ridiculous trying to recapture the fun that we *used* to have. I didn't think that I was that old Ralph, but you've shown me that I was wrong. I just thought that going to amusement parks and dancing and rollerskating was the kind of thing that would keep you young. It might've, at least it was worth a try.

But you don't have to worry Ralph, I promise you you will never have to laugh at me again. I will stop being ridiculous, and I will never, *ever* mention it again!

Alice is steamed because Ralph is too cheap to buy a television set.

Alice: Now look around you, Ralph, we don't have any

electric appliances. Do you want to know what our electric bill was last month? Thirty-nine cents! We haven't blown a fuse, Ralph, in ten years!

Ralph: What ever happened to the sweet, unspoiled girl I married before? What ever happened to that girl, Alice? Do you remember what you said to me before we got married? "Ralph, I'd be happy to live in a tent with you."

Alice: I'm still waiting. I think it'd be an improvement.

Ralph: Do you wanna go to the moon? Do you wanna go to the moon?!?

Alice: That would be an improvement, too. Now let me tell you something, Mr. Financial Security, I want a television set and I'm gonna get a television set. I have lived in this place for fourteen years without a stick of furniture being changed. Not one! I am sick and tired of this. And what do you do, you don't care about this. This place looks like Washington's birthplace or somethin', we gotta *preserve it* exactly as it was. You know what it looks like to me, it's more like Lincoln's birthplace. And what do you care about it, you're out all day long. And at night what're you doin', spending money playing pool, spending money bowling, or paying dues at that crazy lodge you belong to. And I'm left here to look at that icebox, that stove, that sink and these four walls. Well I don't wanna look at that icebox, that stove, that sink and these four walls. I wanna look at Liberace!

Alice is trying to convince Ralph that his latest foolproof scheme is doomed to failure.

Alice: But Ralph, hair restorer! Don't you realize this is in the same category as the times you went in for the phony gold stock and the fake oil wells?
Ralph: Are you gonna throw that up to me at this hour of the mornin'? Are ya, heh?!? Two mistakes!
Alice: How about the goat-gland vitamins?
Ralph: Three mistakes.
Alice: How about the shoe-shine polish that glows in the dark?
Ralph: Four mistakes.
Alice: All right, how about....
Ralph: Why don't you stop!

Ralph has been laid off and the Kramdens have only a few dollars in the bank. Alice's solution to the problem: she'll get a job.

Alice: Now nobody's gonna give you a job, Ralph. Just like you said, they'll find out when the layoff is over you're going back to work for the bus company. But there is no reason in this whole earth why *I* can't get a job.

Ralph: That is out, o-u-t, out. While you are my wife you will never work. I have my pride.

Alice: I'm gettin' a job, Ralph, no matter what you say.

Ralph: I'm not gonna argue with you, Alice, because first of all, what could you possibly do to earn any money?

Alice: Well, there's plenty that I could do, Ralph. I took a commercial course in school, I still remember my shorthand and my typing. I can get a job as a secretary.

Ralph: Oh, you can, heh? And who do you think is gonna do the housework around here?

Alice: Guess?

Ralph: Oh no! No sir! No sir sir sir sir! No sir! Not me!

Alice: Oh yes you are, Ralph. I'm gettin' a job and you're gonna do the housework!

The Kramdens have gotten a telegram from "Mother" and they think that it's Alice's mother who's coming to visit. Ralph, naturally, has blown his top.

Alice: You can yell and scream all you want to, but I want you to get one thing straight — my mother is coming here and my mother is always welcome in *my house.*

Ralph: Your house? Yooouuuuurrrr hooooouuuussse? This is *my house* Alice, m-y house, my house. My house!

Alice: Oh I am sorry Ralph, I forgot, it is your house. You really have been very big-hearted, Ralph, sharing it with me, letting me live here with you in the lap of luxury like this. Don't think that I don't appreciate it Ralph, 'cause I do. After all, where else would I get a beautiful home like this? This place Ralph, you know what it is, it's a regular Disneyland. Look, Ralph, look at this wonderful view that we have from the window. Look, see, old man Grogan's long underwear hanging on the line, garbage cans in the alley, the back of a Chinese restaurant. That's all part of my Disneyland too, Ralph. That is my Fantasyland. Now Ralph, over here, this sink. Every time I go near that sink, Ralph, I never know what's gonna happen. You know what the sink is? That's my Adventureland. That stove and that icebox...that's Frontierland. There is only one thing, Ralph, that is missing from my Disneyland, only one thing...the World of Tomorrow. I have *nothing* from the World of Tomorrow.

Ralph: You want the World of Tomorrow. Alice? You want the World of Tomorrow? I'll give ya the World of Tomorrow! You're goin' to the moon!!!

Alice: Har har hardy har har!

Alice has had a telephone installed and Ralph is throwing a fit.

Alice: I can give you a dozen good reasons why we need that phone.

Ralph: Yeah, and I'll give you a *big* reason why we can't have the phone, we can't afford it!

Alice: Oh Ralph, a telephone isn't a luxury anymore, it's a necessity.

Ralph: A necessity, heh? They put this in this afternoon, I'll guarantee you've been on it thirty times already!

Alice: I made one call Ralph, one call. I spoke to Trixie.

Ralph: Trixie? Upstairs?!? You called her on the phone to talk to her upstairs?!? Whattsa matter, yellin' out the window is too good for you now? What was it, rainin' out?

Alice: Yelling out the window is bad manners.

Ralph: Don't you make any nasty remarks about my mother. She's been yellin' out the window for eighty years.

Alice: Yeah? And before she lost her voice there were more people listening to her than to Amos and Andy. Now you listen to me, Ralph, that phone is staying here. Everybody but us has a telephone. All you've worried about is the money. Well, you can stop worryin' because I'll figure out some way to pay for that phone. I'll just…uh, well I'll, I'll cut down on something.

Ralph: I know what you'll cut down on — my food. That's what you'll cut down on Alice, my food! We'll have a phone but I won't have anything to eat.

Alice: Oh Ralph!

Ralph: Don't "Oh Ralph" me. I'm sick and tired of hearin' that "Oh Ralph". The bills'll get bigger and bigger and I'll get less to eat. I'll start losin' weight. Then do you know what I'll look like?

Alice: Yeah, a human being.

Their husbands are more interested in going out than being with their wives, so Alice hatches a plan so she and Trixie can win back Ralph and Norton's hearts.

Alice: I been thinkin' Trix, and maybe the reason the boys go out so much at night and don't pay any attention to us any more is our fault.

Trixie: Our fault?

Alice: Well sure. Remember the days when Ed and Ralph wouldn't dream of going anywhere without us?

Trixie: Sure…that was before we were married.

Alice: Exactly. Now the whole reason that it happened then was 'cause we used to knock ourselves out to be attractive and to look glamorous for them, and they paid plenty of attention to us in those days.

Trixie: I get it. Alice, the watchword is "glamour", we're gonna dress to the teeth and make a fuss over the boys. Then they'll treat us like they did before we were married.

Alice: That's right, and tomorrow night, Trix, we're not gonna be wives, we're gonna be dates.

Alice's plan fails, and what's worse, Ralph spent the entire evening flattering Rita, the sexy wife of a bus company executive. Alice thinks that maybe that's the kind of woman Ralph wants and she dresses up and "vamps" for him when he comes home the next day.

When Alice finally explains what's going on, Ralph assures her that he doesn't have a crush on Rita and that he was charming her to make an impression on her husband. Alice finds little consolation in that.

Alice: Well, that may explain your being so attentive to Rita, Ralph, but it doesn't explain something much more important. It doesn't explain why in all these years, Ralph, you've never tried to make me feel like your sweetheart or even noticed how I looked. I wish you had an explanation for that, Ralph, oh, how I wish you had an explanation for that.

Ralph: I have got an explanation for it...I'm a mope. But I love you sweetheart, honest I do. You're the greatest.

Alice: Oh Ralph...!

Alice is upset because Ralph has bragged to a newspaper reporter that he's the boss in the Kramden household.

Alice: How could you, Ralph, how could you? Five men, Ralph, five men answered this question and you were the only one to make an idiotic statement like that. Why, Ralph, why?

Ralph: Because I was the only one brave enough to make that idiotic statement, that's why.

Alice: Ralph, do you think if they'd asked me that question I would have said that *I* was the boss?

Ralph: How could you? How could you, Alice? You're a woman, remember that. Women aren't bosses, *men* are bosses, men! They do it all. Men run this world, Alice. Men. They're responsible for the shape the world's in. Men.

Alice: Well I'm sure glad to hear one of you admit it.

Ralph: Just kills you, don't it. Just kills you that you're a woman. And instead of being a leader like a man, you gotta be a follower. That's what women are you know, followers. Men. All the great inventions, men. Men have done all the great things since the beginning of time. Give you a perfect example, there'd be no America if it wasn't for Christopher Columbus.

Alice: There'd be no Christopher Columbus if it weren't for his mother.

THE ESSENTIAL ALICE KRAMDEN TRIVIA

Q. Alice had three jobs before she married Ralph. What were they?

A. She worked in a laundry, as a riveter in the Brooklyn Navy Yard, and she handed out shovels for the WPA.

Q. When Alice has to get a message to Ralph during the day, how does she do it?

A. She goes to the corner of Madison Avenue and Forty-second Street and hands a note to the cop on the beat, who hands it to Ralph when he goes by.

Q. What did Alice call Ralph before they were married?

A. Her "Little Buttercup".

Q. Alice once had the chance to pose for a magazine ad for a sink cleanser. Name the product.

A. Glow Worm cleanser.

Q. Tired of being without "modern conveniences", Alice has a telephone installed in the apartment. What is the telephone number?

A. Bensonhurst 0-7741.

Q. Which of Alice's sisters marries Stanley Saxon, one of Ralph's Racoon Lodge buddies?

A. Agnes.

Q. When did Alice and Ralph have their first fight as husband and wife?

A. Right after the wedding, on the train to Niagara Falls.

Q. What was Alice's affiliation with the Racoon Lodge?

A. She was a member of the ladies auxiliary.

Q. What grammar school did Alice attend?

A. P.S. 73.

Q. What Girl Scout troop did Alice belong to?

A. Troop 35, Red Wing Patrol.

Q. Alice moved with Ralph out of Brooklyn twice. Where did they move to?

A. Flushing, Queens.

Q. What is Alice's favorite appetizer?

A. Sweet and sour lichee nuts.

Q. Alice has a favorite aunt who always came to visit. What is her name?

A. Ethel.

Q. Alice had six boyfriends before she married Ralph. Who were they?

A. Bill Davis, Jack Townsend, Chester Barnes, Fred Beatty, Johnny Farrell, and Eddie Townsend.

Q. Alice and Ralph lived with Alice's parents, the Gibsons, after they were married. How long did they live with the Gibsons?

A. Six years.

Q. What was Ralph's "pet name" for Alice when they were dating?

A. Bunny.

Q. Alice and Ralph were the parents of an adopted baby girl for a week. What did they name her?

A. Ralphina.